BIG CATS

OF MALA MALA

BIG CATS

OF MALA MALA

SUNBIRD
PUBLISHING

First published 2001 by
Sunbird Publishing (Pty) Ltd
34 Sunset Avenue, Llandudno,
Cape Town, South Africa

Registration number: 4850177827

10 9 8 7 6 5 4 3 2 1

Publisher DICK WILKINS
Editor BRENDA BRICKMAN
Designer ODETTE MARAIS OF FLY DESIGN
Consultant PROF J DU P BOTHMA
Production Manager ANDREW DE KOCK

Reproduction by Unifoto (Pty) Ltd, Cape Town
Printed and bound by Tien Wah Press (Pte) Ltd,
Singapore

ISBN 0 624 03893 9

PHOTOGRAPHERS' DEDICATION
To our dear friends – Ken and Paula, Glenn and Paul

AUTHOR'S DEDICATION
To my family, Stan, Eileen and Carolyn, with love

PHOTOGRAPHERS' AND AUTHOR'S
ACKNOWLEDGEMENTS
Sincere thanks to Mike and Norma Rattray for giving us access to Mala Mala –
that very special place – and to Dave Evans for his support and encouragement.
Our appreciation to the rangers of Mala Mala, in particular Chris Daphne
and Quinton Haddon for their help and interest.
A big thanks to Nils Kure for his invaluable assistance, and to the Sunbird team,
Dick Wilkins, Brenda Brickman and Odette Marais; it's been a pleasure working with you.
Our thanks also to Jeff Wardropper and his staff at Photoworld
in Pietermaritzburg for the care taken in processing our films.
We are grateful to Rob More for his input regarding the Shangaan people, and
to Darrel Bristow-Bovey for his help and support.
Finally, thanks to Kim and Annette Wolhuter for sharing their camp with us.

ROGER & PAT DE LA HARPE AND HEATHER DUGMORE

The author would like to acknowledge the following authors and publishers for quotes used in this book:
Memories of a Game Ranger. Harry Wolhuter. The Wild Life Protection Society of South Africa. 1948.
Leopards. Nils Kure. (Pending publication.)
The Leopard. Peter Turnbull-Kemp. Howard Timmins, Cape Town. 1967.
African Nature Notes and Reminiscences. Frederick Courteney Selous. The Pioneer Head,
Zimbabwe. 1969.

HALF-TITLE PAGE Lion, leopard and cheetah have been hailed as mystical totems by kings and
healers throughout the world's history.
TITLE PAGE A magnificent female leopard slowly awakens from a long afternoon slumber.
OPPOSITE A cheetah mother rears her litter alone, teaching her cubs everything they will need
to know in order to survive.

contents

OPPOSITE Despite his powerful and confident bearing, the lion often has a wistful gaze.

foreword

I HAVE BEEN PRIVILEGED to be closely associated with the Lowveld in South Africa from July of 1937, when my father first acquired land adjacent to Mala Mala. In 1964 we purchased the Mala Mala Game Reserve from the Campbell family, who had until 1960 utilised this area for sportsman hunting during the winter months, when all predators especially lion, leopard and cheetah, were generally regarded as vermin and were hunted on sight. It therefore gives me enormous pleasure to write the foreword to the BIG CATS OF MALA MALA.

Roger and Pat de la Harpe are good, old friends of Mala Mala, and they have photographed our cats with unparalleled excellence and professionalism for a number of years. We were approached by them in 1998 with a suggestion to produce a book to record the transition of Mala Mala from a hunting property to photographic destination. I was therefore delighted that the transition from shooting to wildlife photography at Mala Mala would be accurately recorded, especially as this form of sustainable land use over the past 40 years has proved to be very successful.

Heather Dugmore undertook a great deal of the research for the text and she is also highly commended for her accurate and detailed contribution to this book.

It is also very important for us to recognise and thank our neighbour, the Kruger National Park, for its sound environmental management practices, without which Mala Mala would not be able to offer such excellent sightings of Africa's big cats. Finally it goes without saying that maintaining the environmental integrity of Mala Mala is our only aim, and it is because of this commitment that it is possible to view Mala Mala's big cats in their own pristine environment, as is recorded in this publication.

Our sincere congratulations go to the De la Harpe team for an excellent and accurate work of art.

MICHAEL RATTRAY
MALA MALA 2001

OPPOSITE The Sand River at dawn: lifeblood of Mala Mala.

mala mala

In the northeastern corner of South Africa at the foot of the

Great Escarpment lies a wilderness known as the Lowveld.

Over the years, human habitation has carved its inevitable mark

on much of this region, but a handful of people with foresight

has ensured that nature retains its stake in the land, vast tracts

of which remain wild.

AT THE HEART OF THIS WILDERNESS lies big cat country. Situated in the Sabi Sand Game Reserve on the fenceless western boundary of the Kruger National Park is the Mala Mala Game Reserve. Recognised as one of the top safari destinations in the world, here one can more regularly spot lion, leopard and cheetah than in many other places in Africa.

The name Mala Mala has become synonymous with big cats, and the reserve is dedicated to their conservation. It is hard to imagine that only a few decades back, they were in danger of becoming extinct.

It was the foresight of early conservationists such as Wac Campbell, Mala Mala's first owner, that helped to save the big cats. In 1951 Campbell warned that the cats, especially lion, had been shot out to such a degree that they had become scarce in what was then known as the Sabi Game Reserve. Although Campbell was a keen hunter, he was also a lover of wildlife. That year he put a stop to the indiscriminate hunting of lion in the area, first banning the shooting of lionesses. In time, all hunting was banned in the area.

Today, big cat numbers in the Sabi Sand Game Reserve and adjoining Kruger National Park have been successfully restored, and it is estimated that the region is currently home to about 1 000 leopard, 2 000 lion and 200 cheetah.

The Kruger National Park and Stevenson-Hamilton

The value of the Lowveld's abundant wildlife has not always been appreciated. By the mid 1800s, the area had established itself as a popular hunting ground for ivory, horns, skins and trophies.

In 1884, Paul Kruger, president of the Transvaal Republic, concerned by the devastating wildlife losses suffered in the Lowveld, decided to take action. In 1898, the first government-declared game reserve in Africa was created: the Sabi Game Reserve. Mala Mala – the Shangaan name for sable antelope – was listed as farm number 384, in the centre of the reserve.

Taking up his post in 1902, the reserve's first warden, Colonel James Stevenson-Hamilton, was horrified by what he saw. The Sabi Bridge area, once 'red with impala' that had, in turn, encouraged the presence of their big cat predators, was barren of game.

'No hunting ethics existed whatsoever. If a man did not succeed in killing an animal he had fired at, the next best thing, for his own glorification, was to have wounded it,' said Stevenson-Hamilton. As for the big cats, they were regarded as vermin, killers of creatures which should rightfully belong to the human predatory animal; when shot they were generally left where they fell.

Stevenson-Hamilton dedicated himself to the conservation of wildlife for the next 44 years. It was no easy task, and he searched far and wide for an assistant to help him in the struggle to preserve big cat country.

Harry Wolhuter was a farmer and hunter from the Logogote region, just outside the boundary of the new reserve. Wolhuter was a crack shot, but did not believe in reckless killing. He was also fluent in the local Shangaan language, and was well liked and respected by the Shangaan people, as well as being a master of bush lore. Stevenson-Hamilton had found his man. Together they fought endless battles against poachers, developers, officialdom, disease and drought. Under their supervision, the Sabi Game Reserve began to flourish.

Mala Mala benefited greatly from their enterprise until 1926, when the boundaries of the reserve were expanded and the Sabi Game Reserve was renamed the Kruger National Park. The north–south boundaries were extended and the western boundary was drawn eastwards by 15 miles, positioning Mala Mala outside the new park.

Cattle-ranching

Despite the changes, the wardens of the Kruger National Park continued to play a vital role in the lives of the landowners on its borders. They advised them on game management and discouraged cattle-ranching, then extensive in the area.

Harry Kirkman, manager of the cattle farm, 'Toulon', which adjoined Mala Mala, had the unenviable task of protecting 500 head of cattle from lion, who found them far easier prey than the swift-moving antelope. Kirkman destroyed over 500 lions between 1927 and 1933. But he, like many other hunters, later turned conservationist, championing the very predators he had persecuted. 'Toulon' reverted to game-ranching, and Kirkman later served as warden of the area for a period of 10 years.

In 1938 the outbreak of foot-and-mouth disease in the Lowveld resulted in the destruction of all domestic stock in the area, thereby ending the cattle-ranching era.

Winter months at Mala Mala

Wac Campbell, who had bought Mala Mala in 1928, was sympathetic to the ranchers' losses, but pleased that cattle would no longer plague the region. A sugar industrialist from Natal, he bought the farm in order to hunt game, but also because he had a keen interest in wildlife management and conservation. All hunting at Mala Mala was carried out under strict rules. Campbell insisted that only solitary animals be shot and was vehemently opposed to the rapid-fire destruction of prides and herds practised in other areas.

However, it was not until the 1950s that the big cats and most other carnivores were recognised as worthy of conservation. Until then, hunters had regarded them as vermin, and shot them without conscience. The 'vermin list' included lion, leopard, cheetah, civet, serval, jackal, hyena, baboon, wild dog and crocodile.

Wac and his posse of hunting pals – among them Loring Rattray, who worked with Campbell in the Natal sugar industry, and dreamed of one day owning a place in the wild – spent many happy days at Mala Mala during the winter months of each year.

On the long journey to the Lowveld, Campbell and the fellows would chat excitedly about the sights that awaited them at Mala Mala: the last of the yellow leaves dropping from the kiaats, and the bateleurs resting on the uppermost branches of bare marula trees.

Evenings were spent around the camp fire, where the men discussed their day, grossly exaggerating the size of the big cat they had pursued, and debating at length about whether it was preferable to be attacked by a lion or a leopard.

Given that most attacks on humans by big cats are out of fear or desperation – usually when the animal is wounded or cornered – their reputation for being notorious aggressors is not to be given any credence. In fact, most big cats would rather give human beings a wide berth.

OPPOSITE LEFT Through the decades, many companionable hours have been spent around the fire in the boma at Mala Mala.
OPPOSITE RIGHT At the turn of the last century, lion hunting was considered a great sport.
TOP Colonel James Stevenson-Hamilton and Harry Kirkman (ABOVE), remarkable conservation pioneers of the Lowveld.

The life and times of those early years was faithfully recorded in a hunting log-book, now stained and curling with age. An inscription from 1930 details the visit of Princess Alice, granddaughter of Queen Victoria, and her husband the Earl of Athlone, who came to Mala Mala that winter to shoot lions. Alec Logan – one of Wac's pals, and a crack shot – was appointed the princess' 'companion'. Together they tracked a lioness, which took some time to locate and position in the good lady's sights. Finding that the princess was trembling with nervousness, Logan stretched out a muscular arm so that she was able to rest her gun on it when she fired.

The royal retinue had a rollicking time in the reserve and shortly after their departure, Wac Campbell received a letter from the princess.

'Dear Willie', it read, 'thank you for an absolutely glorious time …'

Lengthy were her lyricisms about the African bush and her admiration for 'the gallant Alec Logan who proved a man in a thousand.'

A new era

Mala Mala was primarily a male retreat until the camp became more easily accessible, and conditions more comfortable. To this end, in 1937, Wac Campbell's son, Urban, cleared an airstrip in the reserve and flew in by aeroplane.

Two years later, however, all visits to Mala Mala temporarily ceased when World War II broke out. Exacerbated by the lack of manpower at the reserve during the forties, poaching was rife here, as well as at the handful of other game ranches in the area. In an effort to combat the problem, Mala Mala and the surrounding farms combined to form the Sabi Sand Game Reserve in 1950.

At its helm was hunter-turned-conservationist, Harry Kirkman, who proved a most vigilant warden, and was years later honoured for his dedication to the preservation of wildlife when two of Mala Mala's camps – Harry's and Kirkman's – were named after him.

The turning point

In the summer of 1951, Wac and Urban Campbell conducted the first comprehensive lion count; the results were shocking. Mala Mala, home to hundreds of lion 20 years previously, now had only 14.

Before the year was out, Wac wrote the following letter:

'To fellow sportsmen who come to Mala Mala camp.

Several of us have been concerned for some time about the decrease in the lion population. Every year fewer and fewer are seen. We are certain you will agree when we say that the lion makes Mala Mala and should he be eliminated altogether, something which is irreplaceable as far as hunting and interest are concerned will have been lost to us forever. This is the only area left in South Africa where lions are in fair number.'

Wac subsequently put a stop to the hunting of lionesses to allow them to breed. He did not yet regard leopard and cheetah as threatened, because it was difficult to estimate their numbers.

That same year Campbell handed over the running of Mala Mala to his son Urban, who preferred the camera to the gun. Urban expanded the reserve, and began marketing it as a bushveld paradise for photographic safaris. His concept did not enjoy a good reception from some of the other Sabi residents, who considered it 'stinking commercialism', but he knew it would save the reserve.

Tourism had already proved the financial lifeblood of the neighbouring Kruger National Park, which, for survival purposes, had opened its gates to travellers in the 1930s. Local and international tourists streamed to the Lowveld to visit the park. Many hired taxis, and paid the drivers half a crown for each lion spotted. It proved a most profitable business, as the driver, after encountering a pride, would drive the party around the reserve for a few miles, and then bring them back to the same pride by another road!

Opening the doors to tourists proved to be just as financially beneficial to Mala Mala, as tourists and eager wildlife photographers descended on the reserve.

Campbell politely advised photographers against various madnesses, such as approaching fighting animals on foot to capture a good close-up!

Urban successfully ran Mala Mala until 1964, when he sold it to his father's friend and colleague, Loring Rattray, who was finally able to fulfil his dream of owning a wildlife reserve. Loring's son, Michael, took over the reserve on his father's death in 1975.

Michael 'White Zulu' Rattray was just a small boy when he first visited the Lowveld with his father in the 1930s to inspect the farm adjoining Mala Mala.

'It was quite a journey,' he recalls. 'The petrol tank of our old Cadillac broke and our Dobermans – we'd brought them along in the supplies lorry to chase off the lions – ate the chickens en route.

My father was enraged; moreso when I persisted in playing my mouth organ, which he confiscated and tossed into Swaziland. I've been looking for it ever since.'

On that trip, they tracked and hunted lion, but it wasn't until Michael was 25 years old that he saw his first leopard. Even though hunting had been banned at Mala Mala in 1965, the leopards kept their distance, and between 1965 and 1975 only three were spotted in the reserve.

'Very little was known about big cat behaviour at that time. We believed all sorts of strange notions; like that lions roared but not lionesses,' said Michael Rattray, who hung up his rifle many years back.

But the bushveld has a mischievous spirit and patiently waits to play tricks. In 1983 Michael invited Tayi Mhlaba – he was Loring Rattray's chief tracker and had accompanied the young Michael on many a hunt – to the opening of Kirkman's Camp at Mala Mala.

Party guests – primarily conservationists – literally bristled when Tayi, then an elderly man, produced a package from which he retrieved a photograph taken in the 1930s; the image was of a young Michael posing beside the first lion the proud lad had shot.

Tayi altogether failed to appreciate why Michael suggested he rather put it away.

The new millennium

Now in his late sixties, Michael is as robust and active as ever, and it is unlikely he will ever retire. If there are firebreaks to be burnt or roads to be fixed, he's out there in the midday sun, making sure that work is carried out to his stringent satisfaction. Management is diligent, and regular game counts, bush-clearing and, where necessary, culling is carried out to ensure the maintenance of healthy animal populations.

'Wildlife conservation is about sustainability,' states Michael. 'If numbers get out of balance, culling is sometimes necessary. In this case, unlike the hunters, we go for the poorest specimens in the gene pool.'

In the Rattray era, Mala Mala has been transformed from a huntsman's Eden into a game-viewing paradise. The Rattray family has put a lot of effort into the infrastructure of the reserve, and its accommodation and table is world class, but the secret to the reserve's success is Michael's ethos that humans be kept to a minimum in the reserve.

Motivated by his inherent love of the bush, he maintains a regime of minimum interference with wildlife, and animals are left to their own devices for some 66 per cent of each day. During morning and evening game drives, rangers follow the rule of only one vehicle per sighting.

This way visitors are guaranteed a superb game-viewing experience, which is why they come here from all over the world to see Africa's 'gold', the big cats.

OPPOSITE Mala Mala has three camps: Main (LEFT), Harry's (CENTRE AND RIGHT) and Kirkman's.
The latter two are named after the one-time warden of the Sabi Sand Game Reserve, Harry Kirkman.
ABOVE Moonrise over the African savanna at Mala Mala.

big cats

From the brooding spirit of Africa emerge three enduring animals: the lion, regal and powerful; the leopard, elusive and silent; and the cheetah, swift and elegant. They number among the seven surviving big cat species on our planet – alongside the tiger, jaguar, snow leopard and puma.

FOSSIL RECORDS REFLECT THAT four-fifths of the large cats that once roamed the earth have vanished. The lion, leopard and cheetah, in the forms in which we know them today, made their appearance around 3.2 million years ago, at the time when much of Africa's forests and woodlands 'opened up', transforming large tracts of land into expansive savannas. These big cats were successful, with little to impede their procreation until the early 1600s, when Europe began to turn its attention to Africa.

At the time, Africa teemed with wildlife, the big cats being no exception. The indigenous peoples had lived in harmony with wild animals for thousands of years, maintaining a healthy respect for the large predators. But the Europeans brought with them an ignorance of wildlife, and in time their fear of and desire to hunt the big cats led to the indiscriminate destruction of them.

By the mid-1800s, large-scale hunting of the 'big five' in Africa had changed from a sport into an industry, and the continent had become a killing field in the bloody scramble for ivory, horns, skins and trophies. And by the mid-1900s, big game numbers had dropped to alarmingly low proportions. Millions of animals had been sacrificed in the name of the Shaw and Hunter Trophy, the Oscar of big-game hunting. Cat populations plummeted, each year bringing them closer to extinction.

Fortunately, at the turn of the last century, a generation of committed conservationists emerged among the rampant trophy hunters to rescue the big cats and wildlife in general. In recent decades, attitudes towards the big cats have completely reversed.

Today, conservation awareness is growing, and big cat numbers are again on the rise. Leopard – the most adaptable of the big cats – number several thousand in South Africa, and total about 700 000 in Africa.

Some 3 000 lion are found in South Africa, and well over 30 000 in Africa as a whole. The most endangered of the big cats is the cheetah, with only about 1 000 found in South Africa, and about 12 000 throughout Africa, mainly in the east and south.

Consummate predators, the big cats are at the top of the food chain, with the lion at the apex. With its massive, maned head, giant paws, and full-throated roar, the lion is aptly named 'king of the beasts'. Heavy (an adult male weighs between 190 and 260 kilograms) and powerful, a lion can clear 12 metres at a leap, and bring down a wildebeest that is of the same weight.

The king of the beasts harbours few enemies, and its closest competitor is the spotted hyena. Africa's second-biggest carnivore, the spotted hyena is a force to be reckoned with.

An adult female hyena – while fairly insubstantial in comparison to the lion – is capable of running down and killing a wildebeest three times its own weight, and even larger prey species such as giraffe and elephant.

Lion and hyena are frequently embroiled in the game of 'hijacking' one another's kills. Hyena are adept hunters themselves, but will discard a kill

and slink away from a pride of hungry lions as quickly as a lone lion will turn tail when approached by a pack of hyena.

The leopard, for its size and weight – an adult male weighs an average of 65 kilograms, a female 35 kilograms – is an extraordinarily powerful and dangerous predator, yet it will often allow a spotted hyena to take its kill. This is though to be because the leopard is a solitary animal, and will back away from any confrontation that might pose a threat to itself.

The cheetah is the least aggressive of the big cats, and will steer well clear of lion, leopard and hyena. Comparatively lightweight – adult males weigh around 45 kilograms – the cheetah is no match for other large carnivores, which appropriate at least 10 per cent of its kills.

Adept stalkers and killers, the big cats survive on a diet of fresh flesh, although the leopard and even the lion are not averse to eating carrion.

Leopard sometimes 'tree' their kills, dragging prey sometimes twice their own weight up a tree in an effort to escape scavenging lion and hyena. A leopard might tree several carcasses if the opportunity to kill more than it can eat arises and will return to feed on its cache over a period of days. Lion too will feed for up to four days on a large kill, while the solitary and more vulnerable cheetah will 'wolf' down its prey, moving on quickly before it arouses the attention of other predators.

Leopard and cheetah usually apply a stranglehold to their victims' throats, 'suffocating' the prey before digging in for a meal, whereas lion will hang onto a victim with its claws, biting chunks out of a large animal until it falls to the ground, weakened by pain and loss of blood.

The claws of the lion and leopard are sheathed when not in use, while those of a cheetah are only partially sheathed, or semi-retractable, to assist it in gripping the earth while running. The cheetah too has a long dew claw, which is vital when killing prey, and often the only means of securing a victim.

From the earliest human records, the big cats have inspired Africa's superstitions and beliefs.

OPPOSITE As a right of passage into manhood, Maasai youths had to face and kill a lion with a spear.

TOP AND ABOVE Maasai men hoped to acquire a leopard's fearlessness and cunning by dipping their swords in its blood.

This leopard was standing three metres above us in the tree. We stared at her and she stared right back at us. She didn't take fright or run away.'

Many of the Lowveld's big cats are habituated to vehicular and human presence, but in other areas in Africa the cheetah, in particular, is incredibly sensitive to the sounds of an approaching vehicle.

If speed is the cheetah's principal asset when hunting, the lion and the leopard are by no means laggards. The leopard can reach speeds of 60 kilometres an hour over short distances. However, it rarely resorts to sprinting, preferring the technique of stalking its prey, which it does with infinite patience and in complete silence to within four to five metres – pouncing distance – of its victim.

Lion engage in short chases, usually over one to two hundred metres, and only so that they can get close enough to their prey to enable them to spring on their backs. It has been estimated that in the final stages of a chase, a lion may cover 100 metres in six seconds, or 60 kilometres an hour.

All the big cats have catholic diets, and if a cat happens upon an unexpected meal, it won't hesitate to apply whatever strategy comes to

It is a well-known fact that the cheetah is the fastest land mammal, and, aside from its claws, it uses its tail to 'steer' as it reaches speeds of more than 80 kilometres an hour over about 300 metres as it goes in for the kill.

As large as these cats are, each is perfectly camouflaged in its preferred environment, and spotting the big cats even from a high-standing game-viewing vehicle is not easy. A fully grown lion might remain undetected as it lies in the grass just metres away from a vehicle, cleverly obscured from view by the long, tawny winter grasses of the Lowveld. The leopard and cheetah are equally well camouflaged by leafy bushes and dappled sunlight that blends in with their spotted pelts.

In fact, an alarm call issued by potential prey is often the only indication that a predator is nearby. Vervet monkeys chatter hysterically, impala and bushbuck snort nervously, and baboons bark fearfully in the presence of a big cat. Giraffe and elephant with calves exhibit intense agitation when lion are nearby, and may even attempt to chase them off.

Although these signals are usually rewarded if investigated, they can turn out to be nothing but false alarms. An impala, for instance, might set off the others in the herd by snorting at a strangely shaped clump of grass. A more reliable indication is that of one or more hyena hovering around the trunk of a tree. This usually signifies that a leopard and its kill are in the branches above. And, of course, a fresh carcass of a buffalo or zebra will practically ensure a lion sighting, as lion will stay in the vicinity of a large kill for some days.

Roger de la Harpe describes a typical chance encounter with a leopardess. 'I had been scanning a line of tamboti trees when I noticed a branch that "curved" in the opposite direction to the other branches. The "branch" turned out to be a leopard's tail. If you have spent any time watching leopards walk, the curve of the tail becomes instantly familiar.

mind to make the most of the situation. Roger and Pat de la Harpe witnessed a cunning killing strategy first-hand.

'There was a troop of baboons barking and shrieking in the trees near Harry's Camp,' described Roger. 'We noticed that beneath the trees was a small pride of lion – two males and a female. The lion had trapped them in the tree, and now there was stalemate as each group watched the other. Eventually, the lioness slunk off into the grass, leaving the males. One of the baboons, seeing this and feeling safer, came down from the tree. As he did, the female burst from the bush, where she had, in fact, been waiting in hiding, and whacked it with her paw. The baboon was dead in seconds; she snatched it up in her jaws and disappeared into thick bush. To call the swiftness with which she carried out this manoeuvre "a blur", would be to offer a misleadingly slow impression.'

Leopard favour the habitat of dense, riverine bush, and are often enountered in dry riverbed systems, while lion are more likely to be spotted in bushveld savanna, and cheetah on the open plains. Because all have preferred habitats, competition between the cats for the same prey is not usually an issue.

A lion's diet is extremely varied, although the bigger game species, when available, constitute most of it. However, the diet of any predator is dictated by the availability of prey species.

A study conducted on lion in the Kruger National Park and the private reserves that line its western border revealed a food supply ranging from mice and small mammals (1%) to buffalo (4%), zebra (15%), wildebeest (23%) and giraffe (43%). The Kruger National Park's ubiquitous impala comprises only 6% of the diet of lion in this region. This is hardly surprising as even a 70-kilogram adult impala would not provide a sufficient meal for a pride. Just one male needs to eat 25 per cent of its body weight in a single sitting.

In KwaZulu-Natal, where a broad range of prey species is available, the lion's diet would be as varied as it is in the Kruger National Park. However, in Mashatu, Botswana, where there is an abundance of elephant, elephant calves make up a substantial part of the lion's diet. In arid areas, or where larger prey species are rare, lion will eat porcupine: a tricky business, and one that often results in the predator sporting the odd quill. A porcupine's quills are equipped with microscopic barbs that, once embedded in the skin, resist removal. The quills usually fall out once the infected area has festered, but if they don't they can cause serious illness.

OPPOSITE TOP LEFT In ancient Egypt the leopard was worshipped alongside Osiris, god of the underworld. Like Osiris, the leopard thrives in darkness, the rosettes on its coat resembling innumerable, all-seeing eyes. OPPOSITE BOTTOM RIGHT, TOP AND ABOVE The cheetah symbolised courage to ancient Egyptians, who carved its likeness in friezes and other decorations.

Leopard in the Sabi Sand area take 23 different species of prey, and impala form the mainstay of their diet at 78 per cent. Again, these figures are area-specific. In the Matobo Hills in Zimbabwe, scat (faeces) analysis indicates that the dassie is among the smaller prey species taken by leopard, while klipspringer are among the larger, and are most frequently preyed upon.

The cheetah's favoured prey is any medium-sized or small antelope such as impala, steenbok and duiker, as well as guinea fowl, bustards and hares. Cheetah are usually solitary animals, but studies reveal that groups of subadult siblings will hunt larger animals, such as waterbuck.

With the exception of the gregarious lion, both male and female of the other big cats species are solitary, although nomadic members (usually old males, subadult males and females without established territories) have been known to band together in small groups for protection and hunting. Other than under these circumstances, the only contact made between the opposite sexes of leopard and cheetah is during courtship and mating.

Big cats define their respective territories by scent-marking or 'spraying' with urine, and by rubbing a musky anal-gland secretion onto bushes, trees and grass, specifically at their territory borders and in areas within the territory that they most often frequent. Other members of their species can tell from these 'messages' how long ago the animal was there, what sex it is, and, if female, whether she is in oestrus. Along with preventing unwelcome encounters, this serves to advertise the condition of a female ready to mate.

Lion rarely move out of their home range, and are hostile to trespassing prides. Pride members do not necessarily move as one within a territory, but individually or collectively they all make use of it. Prides may split up, reuniting from time to time.

Lion seem to be incapable of recognising one another from a distance. Individuals that have become separated during a hunt, for instance, often appear to survey one another suspiciously when they meet up again.

Positive identification, it seems, is made at close quarters, and possibly only through a sense of smell.

The cheetah's territory appears to be less defined than that of the other cats, probably because of its extensive size and scale. The home ranges of cheetah males overlap to a considerable extent, and they will tolerate other males and females in their territory.

On the other hand, while there may be some overlap of a male leopard's territory with the adjacent territories of one or more females, adult territorial males will not tolerate one another's presence.

In order for lion conception to be successful, they need to copulate an incredible number of times. Because typically only one oestrus in five results in progeny, couples mate as often as twice an hour. Oestrus lasts about four days. Some 100 days later, if mating is successful, the female will produce her litter. Typically, three cubs are produced per litter. Cub mortality is high, with a survival rate of only about 50 per cent, largely as result of cubs being taken by other predators when the females are out hunting. In addition, incoming dominant males do not tolerate the cubs of their predecessors, and will often kill the cubs in an effort to ensure replication of their own gene pool.

In leopard, courtship is generally instigated by the female. A leopardess will wander widely while in oestrus, leaving olfactory clues of her condition, in which case males will actively seek out the receptive female.

Leopard oestrus lasts four to seven days, recurring every 25 to 58 days until conception. During courtship the pair remains in close association, and copulation may be as frequent as every five to 15 minutes. The gestation period is about 90 days, and usually results in the birth of one to three cubs.

Female cheetah generally only come into contact with males in the period just before and during oestrus, which lasts for about two days. The gestation period is 90 to 95 days, and three to four cubs are produced. As with lion and leopard, almost 50 per cent of cheetah cubs will be taken by predators, including larger eagles in the first few months of their lives.

As a result of the high predation rate, female cats may move dens several times to avoid detection.

The big cats seldom interact with other species, with the exception of hyena, and, of course, the ever-present vultures that advertise the presence of a kill to other carnivores. Black-backed jackals frequently hover warily at the outskirts of a kill, dashing forth bravely to occasionally sneak a bite at the carcass.

In the Kruger National Park, lion are the major cause of wild dog deaths, and in the park and, possibly because of this, wild dog and lion tend to occupy different habitats. While wild dog interactions are rare, big cats can be intimidated by packs, as they usually number up to 20 dogs.

In fact, apart from man, the big cats have no serious predators, and reign supreme. It is small wonder then that lion, leopard and cheetah have been adopted by many cultures, past and present, as symbols of strength and leadership.

Folklore, myths and legends

From the dawn of time, lion, leopard and cheetah have crept into the fears and superstitions of man, and have been singled out as regal and mystical totems by kings and healers throughout Africa's history.

In Zulu and Shangaan tradition, the skins of leopard and the claws of lion are worn only by members of royalty and the most loyal of warriors. Behind this custom lies the belief that the wearing of the skins or body parts of the animal imparts qualities of the animal to the wearer.

The Maasai of East Africa traditionally dipped their spears into the blood of the leopard they had killed, in an effort to acquire a modicum of its fearlessness, cunning and skill. As a show of courage and a rite of passage into manhood, Maasai youths had to face and kill a lion with only a spear, and proudly wore that lion's mane as a headdress.

In days gone by, West African warriors known as 'leopard men' performed a highly secretive ceremony in which a leopard was caught and tranquillised. While sedated, a small incision was made in its flesh, and the warrior would either drink the leopard's blood, or mingle it with his own, inexorably bonding the two. On regaining consciousness, the leopard was set free, and the warrior believed that even if he never laid eyes on his cat brother again, they were linked for life. If the leopard died, he would die too; if he died, so too would the leopard.

There are many mysterious associations between African people and the big cats. In some African societies it is commonly accepted that medicine men and women can transform themselves at will into their totem beast; they do not emulate the animal, they *become* the animal.

Body parts of the big cats are also widely used in traditional medicines, or muti, for a range of physical, psychological and spiritual ails.

A large percentage of Africa's people prefer muti to Western medicines, and believe that the body parts of the big cats can endow them with courage, power, invincibility, potency and speed.

These people will consume, burn, or rub into their bodies the chopped up or boiled skin, whiskers, tongue, eyes, heart, fat, testes or claws of a lion, leopard or cheetah, in an effort to attain all or even some of these qualities.

No part of a cat is discarded, and traditional healers will even use the dried bones to divine the future.

Well-known South African traditional spiritual healer Credo Mutwa believes that human beings are instinctively drawn to the lion, leopard and cheetah because they were placed upon the earth by the gods to protect all forms of life from destructive, demonic entities known as Chitawouli, or 'whisperers of death'.

The Chitawouli thrive on hatred, fear and corruption, and are themselves afraid of nothing bar the big cats. It follows that if the lion, leopard and cheetah disappeared from the earth, prolonged spiritual darkness would prevail.

At the core of this myth is sound conservation practice that engenders healthy environmental respect. But the reality is that much of Africa today has fallen prey to the Chitawouli, although there remain islands of hope where the big cats keep them at bay.

Such a place is the Kruger National Park, and the private reserves that flank its western boundary.

OPPOSITE The leopard's spotted coat is well camouflaged in the dappled sunlight that filters through the bushveld's trees.
TOP RIGHT Lion, inherently lazy by day, become bold and aggressive at night as they head out to hunt.
ABOVE Shangaan mothers place their children on the body of a dead lion, ostensibly to absorb its power.

Gloria Ndlovu, sangoma

A cluster of dark specks – on closer inspection, the silhouettes of 10, maybe 15 white-backed vultures – against the bushveld sky provided the first indication that there had been a kill.

'The lions of Mala Mala are watching them now,' Gloria Ndlovu said. 'They have awoken from their long rest under the marula trees, knowing something is dead. They are watching to see where the vultures land. If they are hungry they will investigate.'

Gloria – her surname is Shangaan for elephant – lives in a village on the outskirts of the Sabi Sand Game Reserve. She is a sangoma – a medicine woman – and ministers to the Shangaan people who inhabit this region.

We watched the birds for some time before she bid us enter her consulting chamber, a mud-and-daub hut laced with the smell of indigenous herbs that hung in large bunches from the walls. Beneath the herbs two rows of shelves adorned with multicoloured potions in small bottles lined the wall. An orange ointment labelled 'Ingonyama/Ngala' (the Zulu/Shangaan word for 'lion') occupied pride of place.

'We use that for strength and protection. It is lion fat,' she said, sitting on the floor with outstretched legs, her cheetah-skin pouch in her lap.

Thick, aromatic smoke spiralled from the small fire burning in the centre of the hut, as she sprinkled on an indigenous incense called *imphepu*.

'So you want me to tell you stories about the big cats. There are many stories. Strange stories …,' she said, her voice trailing off.

'I will tell you something that happened not far from here.'

In Africa, where distances are vast, 'not far from here' could mean two or 2 000 kilometres away.

The story revolves around two lion that had escaped from the reserve, and had begun to prey on a certain villager's cattle.

Two local trackers were assigned the task of hunting down and shooting the lion, and they followed the spoor for many kilometres through the bush.

Eventually the trackers came to a clearing where fresh spoor indicated that the lions were nearby.

'The trackers thought, "We've got them at last!"' Gloria exclaimed.

Apparently, the tracks continued through the clearing towards an old thatched hut, where they stopped at the door. The trackers knocked on the door and tentatively stepped inside. There sat two men.

'That was when the trackers turned on their heels and fled,' Gloria said, peering through the flames with fire-flecked eyes. 'You see, both men had deep gash marks on their necks where the cows had gored them trying to fend off the attack.'

We assumed she was being allegorical, but it turned out she was not. She was in no doubt as to the identity of the pair in the hut. 'They were lion-men,' she said. 'Men who can change form from human to lion.'

Gloria laughed and shook her head: 'You think it is strange but we are part of these animals and they are part of us. If you live for many months in the bush, you will feel it.'

Gloria emptied her divining bones from her cheetah-skin pouch onto a mat on the floor, then scooped up the pile with cupped hands, and blew on them, 'to awaken them'. The bones are consulted for every situation – from love affairs to spiritual illness – and each bone symbolises the people and issues in the patient's life. The position in which the bones fall is crucial. If someone is ill, Gloria can determine from the pattern the cause of the disease, and the remedy.

She pointed out the bone of a lion. Because the lion is considered to be the king over all animals, this bone represents the tribal chief in the area. The bone of a leopard is synonymous with wealth, because the leopard is so able a hunter that it rarely goes without food.

Gloria has many 'cat' cures, some more obscure and complex than others. A traditional Shangaan cure for epilepsy or *wutleka*, she describes, involves a piece of lion skin, and pieces of monkey and baboon skin, mixed together and roasted in a broken pot.

The big cats are mystical symbols for Africa's great warrior nations, including the Zulu (ABOVE, CENTRE LEFT) and the Maasai(OPPOSITE). In Zulu tradition, only members of royalty wear the skins of cats, while the mane of a lion once played an important part in the Maasai warrior's initiation. ABOVE, FAR RIGHT Sangoma Gloria Ndlovu lives in the Lowveld, a timeless place where the spirits of the big cats roam.

The crispy skins are powdered down and made into an ointment, which is smeared on the head, limbs and body of the patient.

The limbs are then pulled with force. After the patient has slept, passed water and evacuated his bowels, he is cured.

To confirm the healing, the sangoma fashions the image of a monkey out of grass, smears the monkey with the same ointment, and fastens it to a long rope.

A small boy must then drag the dummy out of the village, pursued by all his friends, who hit the monkey while shouting in Shangaan, '*Hamba Hamba suka lapha!*' which translates to : 'Go away! Go away!'

The small boy runs until he reaches a tree far away in the bush. Here he hangs the monkey from one of the branches, and there it remains, swinging in the wind, the disease thus expelled.

Many regard the powers of muti, and the throwing of the bones as primitive mumbo-jumbo, but is it really so different from the behaviour of guests at Mala Mala, who surreptitiously secure for themselves big cat talismans from the skins hanging in the lounge?

Of course the pilfering of talismans could signify nothing deeper than a holiday memento or a dare. Gloria disagrees: 'When people come to this wild place, they don't want to leave. That's why they take a piece of lion skin or a claw. This way they take the wild place back home with them.'

Many hours had passed by now and darkness had crept inside Gloria's hut. 'Time is round, you see,' she said. 'Day goes, night comes, day returns. What goes away, always comes back.'

And so it is with the loss of belief in tradition among younger African people. 'But that too is changing; one day they will return, wanting to know about the time when we lived among the big cats.'

A brush with death

The Lowveld still has a strong core of people who identify with the mysteries and myths that surround the big cats.

Mala Mala tracker John Sibuye believes the lion is both his saviour and his nemesis. Several years back, he was out tracking lion on foot at midday when he and the ranger, who was carrying the rifle, were separated. At this unfortunate moment, John found himself face to face with a particularly large lion. He thought his time on earth was over, but instead of attacking him, the lion 'sprayed' all over him, then casually walked off, scraping the ground. John now regards himself a marked man.

'That lion saved my life, which means he has the right to take it away whenever he chooses.'

Such are the mysteries and myths of the big cats of Africa. Perhaps it is fiction; perhaps not. Africa is a continent of inexplicable tales; at the heart of many lie the big cats. None can deny that they harbour a magic of their own. To see a lion, leopard or cheetah close up, in its natural environment, is to understand why they form the cornerstone of so many of Africa's myths and legends.

the lion king of beasts

It takes a keen eye to observe the subtle details of lion spoor – when a pride passed this way, how many lion there were, even their gender. Roger's years of experience as a wildlife photographer have taught him enough about tracking to stand him in good stead while photographing the big cats of Mala Mala.

'IT WAS JUST BEFORE SUNRISE on a crisp autumn morning when we came across some lion and leopard tracks on the Skukuza road. The leopard, which appeared to be a large male, was heading south, while the lion – a pride of about seven or eight animals – were moving north.'

Roger and Pat were torn by indecision. While they needed more photographs of leopard, the opportunity to pursue a pride of lion in transit proved more tempting. After following the lion spoor for a couple of kilometres, they came across the pride – five females and three males tucking into a giraffe carcass. Freshly killed, the dead animal's warm belly

emitted clouds of steam into the cool early morning air, presenting a dramatic portrait against the rising sun.

'For hours they gorged themselves, the males claiming the first sitting,' continued Roger. 'The excessive feeding eventually exhausted the lion. Some passed out in the middle of their meal, right there in the stomach of the giraffe, covered in blood and gore, while others tore flesh off the carcass from around them.'

The pride continued to feed throughout the day, with white-backed and hooded vultures circling high above, patiently awaiting their turn to feed. The vultures later settled in the surrounding trees, gloomily eyeing the carcass but too wary to approach.

'We spent most of the day sitting with the lion, the giraffe and the despondent vultures, and returned early the next morning to take more photographs. As the day wore on we began to hear other lion calling in the distance. Just after dark and without warning, a pride of six lion – three males and three females – stormed in on the feast, much to the surprise of the diners.

'Pandemonium ensued as the mother and father of all catfights raged about us. The aggression and naked savagery was simply astounding. And the noise deafening!' recalled Roger.

It turned out that the six lion that had burst in on the others were part of the Charleston pride, and that the area in which the fight took place was their territory. In South Africa's private reserves, rangers have a habit of naming prides and individual animals according to their territories or nearby landmarks. This pride hailed from the Charleston area of the reserve and it goes without saying that they would not tolerate trespassers on their hunting ground.

'The trespassing pride fled in all directions. One of the large Charleston males managed to get hold of one of the smaller intruders that had ducked into the bushes at the rear of the carcass, behind our vehicle, desperately trying to escape.

'It was already quite dark by now, and we could only dimly make out their shapes in the bush, but we certainly heard the furore up close as the fleeing lion was given the hiding of its life. Fortunately, it managed to break free and with great haste headed off, leaving the stage empty for the Charleston pride to feed on the spoils.

'The whole encounter lasted no more than a few minutes, but it felt like hours, hemmed in as we were by the fury and fear around us.

'We've witnessed a lot of violent encounters in the wild, but this was the most astounding yet and it confirmed beyond doubt the lion's raw ferocity and brute strength. But the most frustrating thing of it all was that in all the chaos and with the light fading fast, we did not manage to shoot a single photograph!'

The giraffe carcass lasted for seven days, feeding two prides of lion, a few jackal, hyena and several vultures. All that remained was a section of backbone and a few stumpy ribs.

OPPOSITE LEFT Lion have four digits on the hind feet and five on the front feet, although only four show in the spoor.
OPPOSITE RIGHT Even the king of beasts is besieged by pests, and will snap at bothersome flies.
ABOVE It is not uncommon to see a lion perforated by porcupine quills; mostly, they fall out of their own accord.

'Whenever we drove past that site we marvelled at what we had witnessed,' said Roger. 'It will be difficult to forget that orgy of rage and greed, and how vulnerable we felt, sitting in an open vehicle just a metre from the scene.'

Lion habitually roar for up to half and hour when the sun goes down, and shortly before dawn. Calling and roaring is a means of establishing territorial rights, of making contact with other pride members, strengthening social bonds, and, of course, intimidating rivals or trespassers.

Sitting around an evening fire in the bushveld at Mala Mala, listening for the inimitable roar of a lion, stirs the deepest sense of wild Africa within. Gazing into the flames from which it seems the lion's eyes were forged, seasoned tracker Willis Hlatswayo sighs. 'Most kings lead dangerous, violent lives. The lion is no different. It often looks like he has it all his own way, lazing in the shade for the better part of the day with a full belly and a handsome family. But his life is full of aggression and threat.'

Male lions reach their prime at five years of age, at which point their life's purpose comes into play: to fight for territory and to procreate. If a male is powerful enough on his own, or if he is part of a powerful coalition of males, as he reaches adulthood he will try to kill or expel the dominant male or males of an existing pride. At Mala Mala, a typical pride numbers about 13, with members constantly coming and going, either alone or in groups of three to five. Where lions are plentiful, as is the case here, a single male has little chance of winning or holding a pride's territory, and coalitions are common since they greatly improve the odds. The size of a coalition's territory depends on prey density, and ranges from 20 to 400 square kilometres.

The prime years for males are short-lived. At eight years of age they are already losing weight and mane hair, and it at this stage that the pride's patriarch will probably be ousted. Most lion retain dominance over a pride for only two years, while they live for about 12. Females live for 10 to 15 years.

Newly ensconced dominant males will often kill the cubs of the former dominant male or males. This way they 'force' the females into season as quickly as possible in order to propagate their own genes. It takes a month or two for the females to become reconciled to the new males, and fierce fighting often takes place between them in the interim.

Lionesses come into oestrus every few weeks over a period of five months, without becoming pregnant, following a take-over. When this period of 'sterility' ends, all the females ovulate, conceive and litter at the same time. Synchronised breeding ensures the lowest cub mortality, because there are no bigger cubs to monopolise milk from the lactating mothers. Generally, litters comprise two to four cubs.

In the Lowveld, females start breeding at the age of four – a full year earlier than the males. The usual interval between births is two years.

Lion courtship may be initiated by either of the pair.

Females typically invite copulation by arching the back, while the male offers a mating snarl, described as a sneeze-like grimace. If the female does not respond, he may stroke her with his tongue on the shoulder, neck or back. When the female is ready, she either crouches in the copulatory position, or walks a short distance and then crouches. The male usually mounts her immediately.

During copulation – which may last up to a minute and takes place up to 50 times a day – the female often purrs loudly. Before dismounting, the male gently neck-bites the female, or emits a drawn-out roar.

The couple remain in close association throughout the mating period and will lie down or walk short distances together.

Unlike other carnivores, there is little real aggression between male and female lion during sex. However, when two males are intent on mounting the same female, they are extraordinarily aggressive. At one sighting, two lion fought all night until dawn over a female in oestrus. They staged their battle over a quarter-acre of land, where small trees were uprooted and blood and hair from the two contenders was strewn all over the bush. Neither was willing to concede defeat, even though females can mate with several males over the period of oestrus, and a single litter can produce cubs with different fathers.

Lion are communal hunters and tactics usually involve three to eight lionesses moving in a broad front in an attempt to drive prey into an ambush or block an escape route. Males only hunt out of necessity.

Nineteenth-century African adventurer Frederick Selous wrote: 'There is no doubt that lions know that the head, throat and the back of the neck are the most vital spots in all animals on which they prey. Zebras are almost invariably killed by bites to the back of the neck just behind the ears, or by bites to the throat; whilst they either dislocate the necks of heavy animals like buffaloes, or hold them in such a way that they can hardly help falling and breaking their own necks.'

Lion hunting in groups have a success rate of about 30 per cent, whereas solitary hunters – such as old bachelors – only bring down some 17 per cent of their prey. Feeding hierarchy in a pride is strict, and dominant males traditionally have first option at a kill. They will attack their own cubs and females if necessary to guarantee a good meal, consuming 40 or 50 kilograms of meat at a sitting.

Aware that they are not first in line to feed, despite doing most of the work, lionesses sometimes employ the most guileful methods to secure food. One lioness brought down an impala, raced off and stashed it, returning empty-handed to the pride, where she lolled about with her cubs, giving nothing away. She later returned to secretly feed, and the males were none the wiser.

Willis Hlatswayo compares the lion with Doctor Jekyll and Mister Hyde. 'By day the lion is quite peaceful. But when night falls and the lion starts hunting, he becomes very aggressive and bold.' A pride will spend most of the day at rest, becoming active as darkness descends.

OPPOSITE TOP LEFT Lion feed on a wide range of animals. In the Lowveld, almost half of their kills are giraffe.
OPPOSITE TOP CENTRE AND ABOVE A lioness leaves the pride to give birth, rejoining it with the her cubs when they are around two months old.
OPPOSITE TOP RIGHT The tawny coats of the pride provide superb camouflage against the similarly coloured bushveld savanna.

According to ancient African belief, the explanation lies in the fact that the lion exhibits the combined characteristics of the cow, baboon and leopard. The gentle nature of a cow is evident in the daytime, when one can virtually walk past a resting lion without being harmed; the lion has the cunning of a baboon, and by night it has the stealth and killer instinct of the leopard.

By night a lion is less likely to be detected by its prey, and the ubiquitous impala is an easy and abundant target. However, even an adult impala would not make much of a meal for a hungry pride, and the lion's preferred prey includes wildebeest, zebra, buffalo, waterbuck and warthog, as well as other medium- to large-sized ungulates. However, being opportunistic hunters, lion will pretty much take advantage of anything that comes their way, from small rodents to young elephants.

Darkness is a predator's greatest ally. Mala Mala ranger Nils Kure, who has spent many hours tracking lion at night, states that 'antelope seem to be well aware of the moon and the weather. Under a full moon, one finds large herds of impala standing in the middle of open areas where they can see a predator stalking. On dark and windy nights, these same areas are traps. Consequently they withdraw into thick bush, where they huddle, taking their chances that a prowling carnivore will not stumble on them.'

Because of its power and strength, the lion has always been hailed king of the beasts. The Zulu name for the lion is *Ingonyama*, meaning 'master of all power and flesh'. The Shona people call the lion *Shumba*, or 'the greatest ruler of all'.

Many romantic and mythical tales are associated with this animal whose regal status straddles the centuries. Gathered around the fireside, Zulu elders have, time and again, recounted the tale of King Mageba and the Lion. The story revolves around a young Zulu prince called Mageba, who was a man of great courage, wisdom and knowledge. At the time of his coronation, and contrary to Zulu royal custom, the sangoma announced that King Mageba must don a lion's rather than a leopard's skin. Everyone in the village wondered what was meant by this deviation from the norm, but the warriors obeyed, and set out to hunt a lion. They returned with the skin of a lion, as well as a live cub, with a slightly deformed paw.

The cub became King Mageba's constant companion, and grew into a powerful lion. Then one day King Mageba announced that his lion must be returned to the wild to seek out others of its kind. 'I cannot enslave

OPPOSITE AND ABOVE The most imposing and largest of the African cats, lion are one of the few carnivore species in which there is a clearly apparent difference between the sexes; the male's most distinguishing feature is his mane, the size and colour of which vary enormously from region to region.

another king in my village,' he said, and released the lion deep in the bush. Several years later Mageba's village was invaded by another clan, and the king was separated from his men. He thought it was the end for him, when suddenly a pride of lion burst through the bush, and attacked his foes. King Mageba was dumbfounded that the lion had left him untouched, until he looked more closely at the lion leading the pride, and saw that he had a slightly deformed paw.

Fictional and true-life stories of close encounters survived by men and beast are told many times over around Mala Mala's camp fires.

One of the most exciting true stories is that of Harry Wolhuter, ranger and confederate of James Stevenson-Hamilton. Wolhuter's encounter with a lion resulted in him being regarded by the Shangaan people as having supernatural powers.

With compelling understatement, Wolhuter describes the attack in his book, *Memories of a Game Ranger*.

'Fortune is apt to act freakishly at all times,' he wrote, 'and it may seem a strange thing to suggest that it was fortunate for myself that I happened to fall on top of one of the lions as he was running round in front of my horse. Had I fallen otherwise, it is probable that the lion would have grasped me by the head, and this book would assuredly never have been written!'

Instead of gripping his head, the surprised lion had grabbed Wolhuter's right shoulder in its powerful jaws, and began to drag him away.

'At this point I was certainly in a position to emphatically disagree with Dr Livingstone's theory, based on his own personal experience, that the resulting shock from the bite of a large carnivorous animal so numbs the nerves that it deadens all pain; for in my own case, I was conscious of great physical agony; and in addition to this was the mental agony as to what the lion would presently do with me; whether he would kill me first or proceed to dine off me while I was still alive!'

An adult male lion, it should be considered, weighs between 180 and 260 kilograms. Being dragged along the ground clamped in the jaws of such a beast, its hot breath upon you, is not something many could consciously recount.

'He was purring very loudly, something after the fashion of a cat – only on a far louder scale – perhaps in pleasant anticipation of the meal he intended to have,' continues Wolhuter.

'As our painful progress continued, it suddenly struck me that I might still have my sheath knife! It took me some time to work my left hand round my back as the lion was dragging me over the ground, but eventually I reached the sheath, and to my indescribable joy, the knife was still there!

'I decided to stick my knife into his heart, and so I began to feel very cautiously for his shoulder. The task was a difficult and complicated one, gripped as I was, high up in the right shoulder, my head pressed against the lion's mane, which exuded a strong lion smell. Any bungling in this manoeuvre would have instantly fatal results to myself.

'However, I managed it successfully, and knowing where his heart is located, I struck him twice, in quick succession, with two back-handed strokes behind the left shoulder. The lion let out a furious roar, and I desperately struck him again: this time upwards into his throat. I think this third thrust severed the jugular vein, as the blood spurted out in a stream all over me.

'The lion released his hold and slunk into the darkness. Later I measured the distance, and found that he had dragged me sixty yards. Incidentally, it transpired, that both first thrusts had reached his heart.'

From that day Wolhuter was nicknamed 'lion-hearted Harry'. Unfazed by the incident, he quickly recovered and resumed his duties, which included monitoring the Kruger National Park's lion numbers to make sure they were healthy.

Mala Mala's seven or so resident prides grow and diminish with the passing years. But Nils Kure favours the Charleston pride. On his mantelpiece is the skull of one of the pride's lionesses, her teeth worn right down. She died at the age of 18, a positive indication of the pristine and well-protected Lowveld environment in which Africa's lion thrive.

The lion, as we know it today, was once distributed over the whole continent of Africa, together with parts of Europe and the Middle East. It became extinct in Europe in about the first century AD and has disappeared from North Africa and the Middle East over the last 100 years.

All the big cats have both colour and binocular vision that increases six-fold as the light diminishes. They also have a well-developed reflective layer behind the retina, making their eyes perfectly adapted for night vision. The lion's eye is larger than the human eye, with a diameter of 37.5 millimetres as compared with 23 in humans.

This pride of lion suddenly sat up and stared

into the middle distance when two male

giraffes began to fight. So preoccupied were

the giraffe in their battle for dominance that

they were completely oblivious to the lion.

An adult giraffe carcass provides more than

enough meat to feed a pride of lion for

several days.

The pride members fought over the steaming spoils of the giraffe kill (PREVIOUS PAGES). This lioness (LEFT) had been trying for some time to get at the kill, and had only just succeeded when a male (BELOW) intruded. She showed her displeasure in no uncertain terms, and he got the message.

Spending time with these lions forever destroyed the illusion that they are dignified beasts. Covered in blood and rumen, they immersed themselves in a gluttonous orgy. The manner in which the lions tucked into their feast ranged from indelicate chewing to tugging at the carcass every which way, including sticking their heads between the skin and the rib cage to get at the fat. This fellow (OPPOSITE), his coat soaked in blood and body fluids, suddenly stopped eating and glared at us with cruel, primal eyes.

The lion literally feasted until they fell asleep on top of the carcass (PREVIOUS PAGES). Nap over, they immediately began to eat again. Sunset on the third day, and still the eating continued, though the carcass was beginning to look the worse for wear. Even a lion can only eat so much before it needs to wander off in search of water. We followed two males down to the Sand River (THIS PAGE). In our eagerness to take a photograph our vehicle became stuck in the sand, wedged between one lion in the reeds and this one (OPPOSITE) drinking. A tense time ensued, but we managed to extricate ourselves without having to climb out of the vehicle.

The lion's tongue is incredibly rough, covered as it is with sharp-pointed, backward-slanting papillae. It is an excellent tool for scraping meat off bones, and for administering a solid groom. In the heat of the day, lion relax (OVERLEAF) in shady spots, under trees or in thickets and even reed beds. On a cool day, they will lie out in the open. Lion may spend up to 15 hours a day resting and sleeping.

While lion are most active at night and make the majority of their kills at this time, they are not averse to hunting during the day should the opportunity present itself, as it did with this zebra. When the zebra wandered too close to the resting pride, the lion instantly sprang to life.

This little cub was very brave, as male lions
do not usually tolerate cubs eating at the same
time as they do. The cub became even more
brazen after a while, and eventually climbed
right into the carcass, poking its head out of
a hole in the dead animal's skin. The adult lion
had 'hay fever', and each time he sneezed he
lifted the buffalo's rib cage, making it look
as though the buffalo was still breathing.

These cubs were part of the Eyrefield pride and were gored and killed by buffalo a few days after this photograph was taken. Some weeks later, seven buffalo were killed by lions in a 24-hour killing frenzy. In human terms, it seemed the lions had avenged the cubs …

The lion is a gregarious cat, and there is a great deal of social interaction among members of a pride. This includes mutual grooming (most frequently, of the forepaws) and the greeting ceremony, when two cats will rub their heads together. When resting, lion roll around and lounge all over each other, reinforcing pride bonds (OVERLEAF).

The flehmen grimace of a male lion after smelling the female's urine to test if she is in oestrus (PREVIOUS PAGE LEFT).

The male can be most affectionate when the female is ready to mate. He often initiates sexual activity with a mating snarl, to which the female invariably responds by assuming a crouching position. After mating, he moves off a short distance and she usually rolls onto her back (PREVIOUS PAGE RIGHT).

Cubs begin to follow their mothers on the hunt at the age of about three months (OVERLEAF), but do not actively participate in the hunt until they are fully weaned.

the leopard

There is an ancient African legend which claims that the spots of a leopard reflect the spoor of all the wild animals living around it. And because of this, the leopard is capable of changing into any one of these animals, making it the source of life.

KNOWN LOCALLY AS *INGWE* – meaning 'pure sovereignty' – the leopard has long been revered by the Zulu and Shangaan people, and has played a pivotal role in their societies. Traditionally, only members of the royal family and warriors who had fought nobly in at least of six battles were allowed to wear a leopard skin. Today, however, the custom remains the preserve of the royal family, who turn out in full leopard regalia for formal or holy occasions.

On a practical level, the leopard's adaptability, elusiveness and stealth are its passport to survival, for it is at home in a wide range of habitats, and can exist on the most catholic of diets. It can survive as ably in truly wild areas as it can within a hand's reach of habitation. Because of its extreme adaptability, the leopard's distribution is far more widespread than that of the lion and cheetah, although leopard are probably the least often encountered of Africa's big cats.

'Taking first prize for sheer beauty among the creatures of the wild, what makes this beauty all the more striking is that it is so well camouflaged. In the mottled shade the leopard lies unseen,' says ranger Peter Turnbull-Kemp, who in 1967 conducted one of the first comprehensive studies of leopard.

Regrettably, dedication to the preservation of the leopard, even in this era of conservation awareness, is not universal, and it is still widely hunted as a trophy.

In the early twentieth century, trophy seekers vastly exaggerated the size of the leopard they had brought down. Claims of bagging 11-foot (3.4 metres) leopard were not uncommon, even though the largest male leopard recorded in Roland Ward's *Record of Big Game*, published at the time, measured nine feet (2.7 metres), and the average length of an adult

male is just over eight feet (2.4 metres). Leopard trophies would be weighed in at over 80 kilograms, in spite of the fact that the average weight of an adult male in the Lowveld is 65 kilograms, and a female 35. To defy the truth-telling tape measure, the leopard's skin would be pulled and pummelled, until the carcass was misshapen but longer, while a pair of grubby boots would assist the scale to improve on the weight of the leopard.

Mala Mala put an end to hunting operations in 1965, but it took 20 years of a non-threatening environment before leopards were regularly seen, as they are today. And even then, the leopard's coat is so well camouflaged by the dappled shade of the Lowveld woodland that it is possible to miss one of these magnificent creatures, though it lies before your very eyes. If a leopard does not feel threatened by humans and/or vehicles, however, it may amble out of the bushes, and clamber lazily up

a tree, lolling about for hours on end, apparently indifferent to the intrusion, and providing immaculate viewing.

Night is, of course, the best time to observe this solitary creature. It is believed that a leopard can see clearly in one-sixth of the light that humans require, and the hours after dark are its most active, and are usually spent hunting and marking territory.

'As night falls, leopard, like lion, undergo what amounts to a personality change, becoming far more confident,' explains ranger Nils Kure, who has made an in-depth study of leopards and written a fascinating account of these cats. 'The males start calling to assert their territory, usually three or four deep rasping grunts spaced at half-second intervals. Then they keep silent. Given their position in the pecking order of large predators – before the cheetah but after the lion – it would be ill-advised to alert the lion – for whom it is generally no physical match – to its whereabouts through excessive advertising.'

OPPOSITE While leopards are predominantly terrestrial (OVERLEAF TOP RIGHT), they are very at home in trees, resting in them during the heat of the day, or hoisting their kills high up into the branches, out of the reach of other predators.

ABOVE This six-month-old female was quite relaxed and happy for us to spend the best part of the day photographing her.

Highly territorial, the male leopard will patrol his domain every night, leaving scent-marks and scrape-marks throughout his territory, which is on average some 13 square kilometres in the Sabi Sand reserve. Females are also territorial, but patrol their territories less completely in the first few months after the birth of cubs.

A male leopard maintains tenure over his territory for between five and 11 years, after which time, if he has not reached a natural end, he will usually be chased off by a younger male. Males generally avoid confrontation because when they do fight, it is most often to the death. Females, on the other hand, are feisty creatures and fight more often, although they rarely come into contact, and they too prefer to avoid confrontation.

In fact, the leopard's solitary existence and stealth have allowed the animal to survive where other large cats of Africa have disappeared, even in suburban areas in southern and East Africa.

Males and females generally keep their distance except when mating. Females begin breeding at the age of two to three years, and even the most demure leopardess will become bold and brazen during oestrus.

A female in season will disregard territorial boundaries to seek out a male, and the act itself, initiated by the female, is a rare sight to witness.

Kure, who has seen more leopards mating than most, describes the ritual: 'The female leopard's ears are usually set slightly back and she walks back and forth in front of the male in a sinuous manner, sometimes even thrusting at his chin with her hips. She then lies in front of him, still purring. The male gets to his feet, his ears slightly back. With a somewhat resigned expression on his face he straddles the female and begins a series of thrusts with his pelvis to effect penetration. Ejaculation is immediate on penetration and with this, the male usually bares his teeth and rests them on the back of the female's neck for a moment.

ABOVE LEFT While leopard prey on small to medium-sized mammals, they will also take birds and occasionally reptiles.
OPPOSITE One morning we came across the Selati female and her cub. After resting a while, they moved off and began to stalk something in the grass. We weren't sure if they were hunting or if it was just a training session for the cub.

The whole process takes about three-and-a-half seconds after penetration has been achieved. Then he dismounts. As he dismounts, the female often spins round and swipes at him with a forepaw. The male rears up to avoid her and, at times, leaps back with all four feet off the ground. Both have ferocious expressions. The male then walks off and lies down while the female rolls onto her back with every evidence of satisfaction.'

Directly following the frenzied, one- or two-day mating period, the leopard pair parts company. If mating has been successful, the female will give birth to between one and three cubs after a gestation period of three months. In the Sabi Sand reserve, most cubs are born in December and January, at the same time as the dropping of impala lambs, so that food is plentiful. Newly born cubs are secreted away by their mother for about six weeks. Thereafter, cubs are introduced to their first kill. They start learning how to hunt from about two or three months, but are dependent on their mother for food for at least a year.

It is most endearing to witness the obvious pleasure cubs display towards their mother when she returns from a hunt. She spends about 60 per cent of her time with the newborn cubs, only leaving them to hunt, sometimes for up to 24 hours at a time. On rare occasions, a male may be spotted with a female and her cubs. Cubs are expelled into the wild at about 18 months, when the mother is due to give birth to her next litter.

She will tolerate the temporary return of male cubs from her previous litter, but two-year-old females attempting the same may be viciously attacked because they are regarded as rivals.

Leopard cubs are far more independent than lion cubs, and will stalk anything that moves – from siblings to squirrels. Lion cubs learn to hunt by following the pride, and the process takes some two to three years, whereas leopard cubs have an innate hunting sense. They do not accompany the mother on hunting expeditions, but develop into keen hunters by the time they reach one year of age.

Kure puts it this way: 'Deep in their feline memory is an incredible, in-built aptitude for hunting, especially developed in young females. Enthusiastic and realistic hunters, they are quick to avail themselves of any opportunity that presents itself, but ignore large and potentially dangerous prey. Males, on the other hand, appear less serious about the business of hunting and waste a lot of time with impractical ambition or wishful thinking.

'Every male I have seen maturing has shown a fascination for buffalo. The youngest leopard I've seen harassing a buffalo was one year of age. He followed the herd for hours on end, taking foolhardy risks.'

Leopard will eat virtually anything, including carrion, and have a robust digestive system that can cope with any amount of putrefaction. Their preferred diet in the Lowveld, however, is medium-sized antelope, and includes impala, duiker and bushbuck. Contrary to popular belief, baboon are not the leopard's favourite food, although leopard are the baboon's most common predator. Judging by the way in which leopard will consume a baboon it has killed, they clearly do not find them tasty, and often abandon the carcass half-way through. Adult male baboon – with canines longer and sharper than a lion's – are also dangerous to leopard, and will gang together to attack the cats, especially if they go for baboon females or young within the troop.

Roger and Pat had a most amusing experience with a leopard and a baboon. 'We were following a young male leopard one evening. He was very relaxed and appeared to be entertaining himself, stalking the occasional rustle in the bush and breezily sniffing trees. At one point he got serious, though, and crouched low behind some tall grass, wiggling his hindquarters in preparation to pounce. Seconds later he leapt high into the air, over the grass, and onto some poor, unsuspecting frog or mouse.

'What he hadn't seen was a very large male baboon sitting on a rock a few metres away, and, of course, the baboon had not, up until this point,

seen the leopard either. Both got the fright of their lives. The baboon was the first to regain its composure and, barking loudly, it bounded towards the leopard, which backed off several metres. Encouraged by this retreat, the baboon put in a full-blown charge and the leopard, deciding that discretion was certainly the better part of valour, moved off with speed.'

The leopard is a cunning hunter, and its most important predatory senses are sight and sound, while the element of surprise is its greatest attribute. A leopard will stalk in complete silence, and is infinitely patient. Generally, a leopard will stalk prey to within four-and-a-half metres before pouncing, taking the animal completely unawares. The maximum distance from which it will spring is 18 metres, and it will abandon a chase within 45 to 100 metres if the initial pounce is unsuccessful, even though it can accelerate to 60 kilometres per hour. If the pounce is successful, the leopard will strangle its prey, locking the animal's throat between its powerful jaws until the last tremor of life subsides. In this manner, the leopard also prevents its victim from emitting a distress call that might be heard by passing lion or hyena. Hyena have a habit of trailing leopard. If a leopard senses its kill is in danger of being scavenged, it will quickly drag it up a tree out of the reach of would-be thieves. An adult leopard is capable of dragging a 70-kilogram impala up a tree.

Leopard exhibit definite 'personalities'; some are clearly bold and bloody-minded, others are tranquil or timid. Having spent many years at Mala Mala, ranger Leon van Wyk is familiar with each resident leopard's individual 'personality'.

'It's scientific taboo but you cannot help developing affection for certain individuals. A particular favourite of mine was a leopard we referred to as the "Jakkalsdraai male". He was smaller than your average adult male, but psychologically stronger, and established himself as the dominant male in the southern part of Mala Mala.'

After seven years of tenure, this leopard was still doing well when Van Wyk returned to the Jakkalsdraai male's territory, after spending some time away from this part of the reserve.

'When I finally came south again I was really looking forward to seeing my old friend, now about 11 years old. Other rangers who had seen the Jakkalsdraai male said they thought he was on his way out because he was no longer marking his territory, but I thought, "that doesn't sound like him," convinced he would do fine for at least another couple of years.'

But when Van Wyk set out in search of him, he found no tracks. He was about to turn round when he spotted four hyena feeding in the heart of the Jakkalsdraai male's territory. 'I was shocked. I was sure the hyena's prey was my friend.' Van Wyk radioed the other rangers, and told them what he suspected, but no one was prepared to come out to confirm the sighting. The Jakkalsdraai male was a favourite amongst all and the radio fell silent. After some time, one of the other rangers arrived, and together he and Van Wyk chased the hyena off the kill to examine the carcass.

'Imagine my embarrassment when, on closer inspection, the kill turned out to be a leopard-print cushion that the hyenas had pinched from Harry's Camp!'

Happy to be mocked by his colleagues if it meant that the Jakkalsdraai male was still alive, Van Wyk again went off in search of the leopard, and later that afternoon found its tracks in the riverbed.

'I don't think I'll ever live that one down,' he adds. 'Years later, when I spot a leopard the guys still give me a hard time. But ever since then I decided that when the Jakkalsdraai male finally does die, it will be time for me to leave Mala Mala.'

The Jakkalsdraai male was last seen in the vicinity of a female and her cubs, and so far there's been no evidence of the leopard's demise.

'So I'll stay,' smiles Van Wyk.

OPPOSITE While leopard easily survive in areas of little or no water – attaining most of their moisture requirements from their kills – they drink regularly when it is available.
ABOVE A leopard's eyes show a wide range of emotions: from baleful and dreamy to cold and furious.

Leopard have particularly well-developed sight, and they may use elevated vantage points to observe the surrounding terrain for signs of game. On sighting a herd of impala, leopard appear to carefully assess the situation, and once deemed favourable, will begin stalking the herd, displaying considerable patience and self-control (OVERLEAF).

The storing of larger mammals in a tree requires great strength. While impalas weighing 70 kilograms are regularly hoisted up trees by leopard, there are records of the these cats doing the same with young giraffe weighing 100 kilograms.

Leopard characteristically drape themselves over branches in trees (OPPOSITE), sometimes in the most uncomfortable-looking positions, and promptly fall asleep.

The most noticeable indication of sex lies in the male's larger forequarters and head (LEFT). We came across this hyena staring longingly up into the tree, investigated and spotted a leopard with its kill (BELOW).

Leopard usually start to feed by plucking the hair from that part of the prey they intend to tackle first (OPPOSITE). They dislike fur and feathers, and rid them from their mouths with violent head-shaking.

The leopard's white whiskers are particularly long and, together with two extra-long hairs in the eyebrows, assist the cat in avoiding obstacles when moving about at night.

We waited patiently with this female leopard (OVERLEAF) until her thirst and the heat of the day drove her to water. Heavy rain from the night before had left a convenient puddle in the road.

This cub, the daughter of a leopard known as the Kapen female, was very relaxed in the presence of cameras and vehicles, unlike her mother, who slipped into the undergrowth the moment we arrived.

Leopard are identified by their spot-markings and their whisker patterns are also individual to each cat.

At Mala Mala, leopard are named according to the territories or rivers in which they hold tenure.

Subadult males regularly stalk large animals beyond their reach; this leopard was treed five times by buffalo, and kept returning for more. This leopardess (OPPOSITE TOP) was annoyed by our presence, and glared at us over the remains of her kill.

A young male (OPPOSITE BOTTOM) stood up and watched a troop of monkeys in a nearby tree with great interest. The monkeys had spotted him first and were chattering in alarm.

The donga systems at Mala Mala are a popular habitat for leopards as they offer thick bush cover for relaxing and resting, as well as providing camouflage for hunting.

On many occasions, when we were following a leopard and it tired of our presence, it would head for the nearest donga and, within seconds, disappear without trace.

In camp one morning, we heard the alarm calls

of vervet monkeys from across the Sand River.

On investigation, we found a female leopard

staring up into the branches of a jackalberry

tree full of very agitated monkeys.

She had already caught one of them and

proceeded to eat it.

Contrary to popular opinion that leopard

do little more than sleep and yawn during

the day (OPPOSITE), they are indeed active at

this time, but their movements are slower,

interspersed with frequent rests.

This young leopardess had her sights set on a herd of impala. We watched her stalk them for half an hour, but she still had a few tricks to learn before bringing one down.

A leopard's hunting instincts are extremely well developed. Cubs will stalk and pounce at small game such as insects and lizards from the age of six weeks, honing their innate hunting skills (RIGHT).

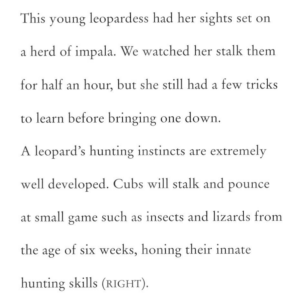

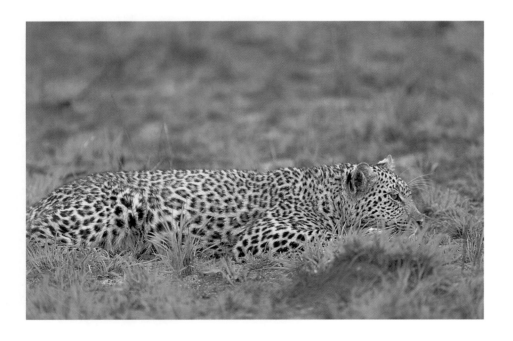

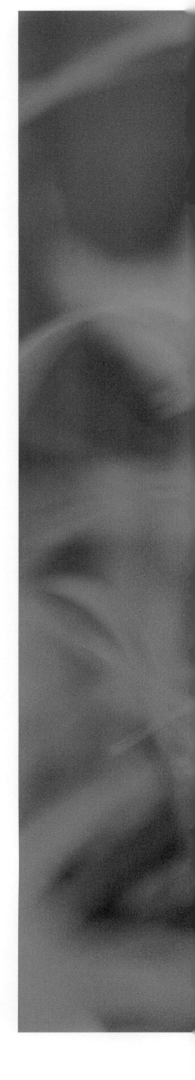

Young female leopard are very enthusiastic hunters, with an aptitude superior to that of males. They are quick to avail themselves of any opportunity that presents itself, but ignore large and potentially dangerous prey. The leopard's spots form rosettes on its flanks and are solid and smaller on the face and underside. The ears are dark at the base with a light patch towards the tips, considered to be a focal point for young leopard following their mother. Males are visibly heavier than females.

This sequence featuring a young male leopard and a buffalo herd was one of the highlights of our year at Mala Mala. Like all young male leopards, this one had no idea of its size and hunting ability, and was intent on catching adult buffalo. The herd became increasingly agitated and we wondered why this clumsy youngster was unsettling them so. Only then did we see that less than 100 metres away, a buffalo calf was being born.

Both male and female leopard scent-mark their territories. With tails raised, they generally spray medium-sized leafy bushes, repeating the exercise every 40 or so metres, but the proximity of scent-marks may range between one and 100 metres apart. On occasion, they will also claw trees and scrape-mark the ground throughout their territories. One leopard at Mala Mala, over a distance of 791 metres, scent-marked 18 times and scraped 11 times.

Destined to become the finest-sighted of animals, the leopard is born blind (PREVIOUS PAGES). The first few days are spent in darkness in the company of as many as five other cubs. Early mortality is high and often only two of the cubs survive. The mother first brings them meat when they are about 65 days old. Suckling continues for about three months. From then until they are about 10 months old, the cubs are led to the kill. Cubs have to hunt for themselves from about a year-and-a-half, when their mother abandons them to give birth to her next litter.

Life in the bush is never boring for a young leopard (THESE PAGES). Subadults spend hours leaping about, chasing whatever they see or imagine they see, climbing trees, leaping from branch to branch, then bounding back down to the ground for a brief rest in the soft grass (OVERLEAF).

the cheetah master of speed

Around 10 000 years ago, at the end of the last Ice Age, many of the world's large mammals became extinct and the cheetah very nearly disappeared with them. Evidence suggests that at that time the cheetah population was reduced to no more than a few hundred individuals.

TODAY CHEETAH NUMBERS ARE AGAIN on the decline, largely due to increasing human populations and the resultant shrinkage of the cheetah's vast habitat requirements. The average male cheetah's territory spans up to 1 500 square kilometres. As a result, there are roughly only 250 cheetah in all of Kruger and its neighbouring private reserves; 'roughly' because taking a census of cheetah is a tricky undertaking as both males and females are semi-nomadic, and their territories overlap. Also, as with any large predators, their numbers vary according to abundance of prey and the presence of other competitive carnivorous species.

What has been established, however, is that since 1900, cheetah numbers in Africa have decreased from 100 000 to about 12 000, the majority of these living in East Africa and southern Africa. Namibia has the largest remaining population of free-ranging cheetah: between 2 000 and 3 000.

Cheetah favour open landscapes, and are well adapted to living in arid environments. They can cover distances of over 80 kilometres between drinks of water, and much of their moisture requirement is consumed in the form of blood taken from prey.

Namibia's cheetah population is spread over 275 000 square kilometres of livestock farmland. This has not been conducive to their survival, as for decades their fate has rested in the hands of the many farm owners who perceived them to be a threat to their livestock. Namibian farmers claimed that cheetah consumed 10 to 15 per cent of sheep and goat stock every year, as well as three to five per cent of cattle calves, and it is estimated that between the years 1990 and 2000, farmers destroyed over 8 000 cheetah.

Much to the relief of the conservation world, a handful of notable initiatives emerged to save the cheetah. One was the 1990 launch of the Cheetah Conservation Fund in Otjiwarongo, northern Namibia, by American Laurie Marker. Marker convinced farmers that there was a workable solution to the problem, in the form of the Anatolian shepherd

dog. Since the introduction of the dogs to Namibian farms, these dogs have prevented the loss of livestock to cheetah, leopard and jackal.

It has taken 10 years, but, as a result, the reckless shooting of cheetah in the area has been considerably reduced. Unfortunately, cheetah are also prized by poachers and illegal wildlife traders. Cheetah have also been captured and kept as pets and for sport for hundreds of years, particularly in Northern India. Even today, young sheikhs from the United Arab Emirates rear cheetah as pets, for racing or to hunt gazelles in the desert, and it is estimated that 100 cubs – averaging about three weeks in age – are smuggled into the Emirates every 18 months by illegal traders.

With its long legs, small head, light bones and slow heartbeat, the cheetah is designed for speed. If it comes within 30 metres of its prey species – mostly small and medium-sized antelope – the prey has most likely lost the race. The cheetah is capable of reaching speeds of more than 80 kilometres an hour over short distances. Coupled with this phenomenal gift is the cheetah's ability to accurately and sharply change direction at high speed.

On one of their many photographic outings, Roger and Pat spent several days with a cheetah female who, under trying circumstances, went hunting for food for her two subadult cubs.

'We spent the morning with the cheetah, who was quite happy to while away the hours with her playful offspring. But we knew that sooner or later she would have to hunt,' explained Pat.

Sure enough, that afternoon the mother suddenly rose from her resting place, completely alert, and headed off, leaving her cubs behind.

'She began stalking a nearby herd of impala she'd seen approaching, but the cubs, instead of remaining behind, followed her and blundered in on her plan. Impala scattered everywhere and the opportunity was lost.

OPPOSITE Two 18-month-old cheetah, brother and sister, played tag in the bush early one morning. They bounded all over the place while their mother looked on. Not long after, she abandoned them in preparation for her next litter. ABOVE Cheetah cluster around a carcass, silently gulping down as much as possible lest a stronger predator arrives and dispossesses them of their kill.

'The mother, heartened by her male offspring's courage, or so it appeared, headed off again to hunt.'

A few weeks after this encounter, Roger and Pat met up with the trio again, a kilometre or two from the area in which they had last seen them.

'This time the family was relaxing under a tree,' said Pat, 'when all of a sudden the young male began stalking something in a nearby thicket. As he got within a few metres of the bushes, a hyena rushed out, with the young male cheetah giving chase.

'The other two cheetah leaped up and joined in the aggressive dispatch of the hyena, which sulkily slunk away.'

The cheetah dispenses of its prey by strangulation. Cheetah don't scavenge, and their preferred prey includes small and medium-sized antelope and hares.

Typically, cheetah stalk prey, stealthily approaching in a semi-crouched position, and freezing mid-stride and dropping to the ground in a crouch if the animal looks up.

The final rush takes the form of a high-speed chase, often over several hundred metres, during which the twists and turns of the prey are relentlessly followed. The acceleration, once the cheetah commits itself, is astonishing to witness. As the cheetah gains on its prey, it hooks the animal's back leg with its dew claw, and pulls backwards. This causes the prey to lose balance and tumble over.

Experienced cheetah capture about 60 per cent of their prey.

Some chases are abandoned almost before they begin; for instance, if the intended victim snorts a distress signal before the point of chase, any competitive predator within earshot of the distress signal will have been alerted and will investigate.

Mom tried a few more times during the course of the afternoon, but on each occasion the cubs alerted the prey. Finally, she managed to give her cubs the slip and brought down a young impala. She immediately called her cubs to come and eat dinner. For once they obeyed but were a little slow on the uptake.

'Before any of us knew what was happening, a hyena rushed in from nowhere, grabbed the impala and disappeared into some thick bush,' continued Pat. 'The mother and cubs were left standing there bewildered. We could feel her frustration as she lay down to recover.

'At this point, another hyena charged out from the thick bush into which the other had disappeared, and approached the cheetah, obviously looking for food.' Hyena are more powerful than cheetah, and do not fear these cats in the least.

'But the male cub, irked by the intrusion, arched his back, started "hissing" madly, and ran at the hyena! Not expecting such aggression, especially from one so young, the hyena backed off with its tail between its legs, disappearing into the bush.

Even if the cheetah does bring down the prey, it is likely to be snatched by a more powerful lion or hyena.

Cheetah hunt predominantly in the daytime. Sleek, elegant and quick as they are, cheetah are timid creatures and even vultures, baboon and jackal can chase them off their prey.

Female cheetah begin breeding from the age of about a year and a half, and engage in a complex courtship ritual. During her two-day oestrus, the female will allow males to approach close enough to smell her vagina. When thoroughly excited, they mock-charge the female, who reciprocates the action.

At this stage, copious urine-spraying may occur, and the males may engage more actively than normal in scraping up small amounts of earth with their back legs, and urinating or defecating on the mounds.

One of the males in the coalition is dominant and monopolises most of the mating opportunities, though courtship fights between males – they rise up on their hind legs and spar with their forelegs – often occur. Male cheetah coalitions maintain tenure for several years.

To initiate copulation, the female arches her back. Both she and the male are very aggressive when he mounts her. He grips the skin of her dorsal neck very tightly in his teeth and thrusts rapidly about 20 to 30 times in succession, before relaxing his grip, dismounting and walking away.

The gestation period is between 90 and 95 days. While the average litter size is three or four cubs, it is not uncommon for litters of eight to be born. The period between births is about 18 months.

As with any of the big cat species, cub mortality in cheetah is high, with predators accounting for over 70 per cent of cub losses in the Lowveld area, largely because cheetah mothers are ineffectual at driving competitors away. In areas where other large predators are absent, the percentages of cub survival are much higher. Often, though, the cubs simply starve to death. Unlike dominant male lion, cheetah males will not kill the cubs of their own species. Cubs that survive the first three months of life stand a good chance of reaching adulthood.

Cubs are weaned at about two to three months, becoming independent of their mother at anywhere between 16 and 20 months. Young females separate from their littermates and avoid contact with other cheetah, except to mate, whereas young male littermates may stay together for life, forming coalitions to secure territorial tenure and facilitate hunts. Cheetah are the most endangered of the big cats; they can, however, live to up to 14 years if they survive the first few vulnerable months of life and the many threats that follow them into adulthood.

Any further decrease in Africa's cheetah population could jeopardise the survival of this already dwindling species. It is our shared responsibility to ensure their survival.

As naturalist George Schaller so aptly put it, 'future generations would feel truly sad that we had such lack of foresight, such lack of compassion, so little sense of future, as to annihilate some of the most beautiful species this planet has ever seen.'

OPPOSITE LEFT These cubs watched their mother intently as she inched towards a herd of unsuspecting impala some 300 metres away.
OPPOSITE RIGHT Encounters between cheetah and spotted hyena are frequent. Cheetah are usually intimidated by the stronger predator.
ABOVE AND OVERLEAF A cheetah and her two cubs lie up in the shade and watch a passing giraffe.

The cheetah's large, copper-coloured eyes are shielded by a membrane during sprints, while its large nostrils allow for rapid oxygen intake. During a chase, its heartrate speeds up dramatically to assist rapid breathing.

The dark tearstains, running down from the inside corners of the cheetah's eyes, are thought to reduce glare.

Lithe and lean, the body of the cheetah

is as long as a leopard's but higher on

the legs, which are thin and muscular. The

tail, long and thick, is used as a rudder to

counterbalance the cheetah's weight while

making sharp turns at high speed.

This cheetah family had gone without food for several days when the mother made an opportunistic kill. She called the cubs over with a bird-like sound, and they all attacked the carcass with relish.

At birth, the cheetah cub's back is covered with a cape of long, bluish-grey hair that disappears when it is about three months old. The bond between a mother and her cubs, and between siblings, is particularly strong. There is plenty of mutual affection and grooming, and they purr loudly when content and during play.

This most uncharacteristic encounter between cheetah and a hyena (OVERLEAF LEFT, saw the hyena backing off, following an aggressive encounter with the young male.

More often than not, however, hyena make off with cheetah kills (OVERLEAF RIGHT).

Cheetah are terrestrial animals, ill-adapted to tree-climbing, but they do make use of trees with stout-sloping trunks or branches, as well as termite mounds and large rocks, for resting and as observation posts.

It is most unusual to see a cheetah kill at night
when the other large predators are active.
This one killed an impala just as the light was
fading. He gulped down big chunks of meat,
constantly checking his surroundings.
Later, two hyena arrived and snatched the kill,
by which time the cheetah had already had a
good feed.

The cheetah's high-domed skull gives the animal its characteristic rounded head. The canines (OPPOSITE) are short, sharp and rounded: their function is to hold the prey by the throat until it has been strangled. They do not use these teeth for severing the spinal cord at the nape of the neck – as other predators do – hence length is not an issue.

These cubs (THESE PAGES AND OVERLEAF) played constantly, stalking stones, hiding from each other behind tree stumps, licking, biting and tumbling over one another.

They occasionally returned to their mother for comfort, while she kept a sharp lookout for danger. The cubs, by contrast, were oblivious to life's hazards and provided us with much amusement for a couple of days.

Cheetah cannot roar. They growl, hiss, yap, yelp and chirp at one another like birds. Their wide communication repertoire is used in many and varied situations, including a mother calling to her cubs, cubs calling to one another, or a mother instructing her cubs to freeze or hide.

A female cheetah's home range may contain

three or four male territories. She may mate

with any of these males, as well as others

passing through. Unlike lion, male cheetah

have never been known to kill cheetah cubs,

perhaps because they have no way of knowing

whether the cubs are their own offspring.

Cheetah as a group have little genetic diversity.

(PREVIOUS PAGE AND THESE PAGES).

Cubs spend about 18 months with their mothers, during which time they learn how to survive (THESE PAGES AND OVERLEAF). It may take them another year or two to become good hunters. They often start out by chasing inappropriate prey such as buffalo, but soon learn that smaller prey species – notably young antelopes and hares – are more within their range.

A real grump bag. A gale was raging this day and a cheetah and her tiny cubs were taking refuge in some thick bush. Frustrated at being cooped up for hours, this cub climbed up onto a tree stump and glared at us as though it was all our fault.

The most delicate of the big cats, the cheetah's

biggest enemy is man. Ultimately, it is up to

us whether they survive as a species or die out

in our lifetime.